LEMUR

Andra Rotaru

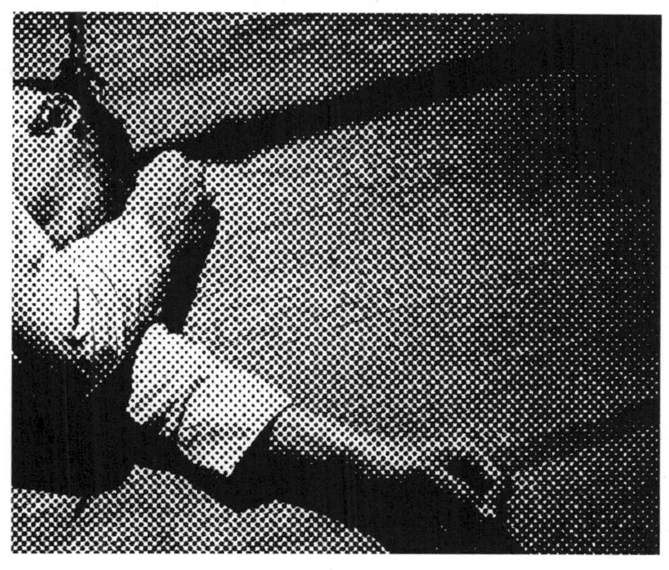

ACTIONBOOKS

Notre Dame, Indiana 2018

Action Books
Joyelle McSweeney and Johannes Göransson, Editors
Jean Yoon and Anne Malin Ringwalt, 2017-2018 Editorial Assistants
Andrew Shuta, Book Design

LEMUR

ISBN 9780900575761

Library of Congress Control Number: 2018937814

First Edition

Photographs pages 75-77 courtesy of Miroslav Milos
Photographs pages 78-79 courtesy of Rebecca Steele

Action Books is housed at the University of Notre Dame, Department of English,
356 O'Shaughnessy Hall, Notre Dame, Indiana, 46556

Visit us at actionbooks.org.

Lemur

by Andra Rotaru

translated by Florin Bican

I. 75 mg

Lemur

he smears butter all over himself,
the texture soaks into the wrinkles of the flesh;
it takes a while until the quickened pores
gape even wider apart,
until their wombs erupt with new flesh,
fervent flesh,
until the torso merges
with the organs.

face to face we are watching each other –
the blood crust connects us
all the way to the wrists,
lips longing to be there,
for a vague moment or two.

you do not exist, I have told you today;
I do believe you are an incarnation of my psychic state; don't laugh,
by tomorrow we'll split,
I love you,
at times, you know it yourself.

*

there was not enough room inside me for the sliver of pill
not to crunch; I'd take it each morning,
for a spell we'd be watching
each other in the mirror:
I'd circle my neck with my palms
and study the way the 75 mg make their progress
along the trachea. the diminutive hump at the base of my neck
was reminiscent of a hill excavated in midfield.
it ceased resembling a landform
in a matter of minutes. within that particular time spanat that precise moment
my throat weighed no more than 75 mg.
about ten percent of what a prosimian might weigh.

with one chunk of animal swallowed each
morning, all these might well shift
into a state of excessive wellbeing:
extreme anxiety levels. He'd know he was right:
looks like orgiastic-anxious syndrome.
imminent relapses would be made up for
with a further few mgs.

Day 1

he stumbled upon me in bed, the top of my pajamas distended, knees pulled up to my mouth

Day 2

nothing at all

Memories

he cannot know so he doesn't answer.
it looks like one of those dangerous games
with animals waiting on both sides
of the barbed wire.

for him they go by different names: first death,
accident next and then murder.
in their wake: suicide, abuse, transformation.

where I come from, they have been
packed with care:
years on end in a body that now
breathes for a few hours.
it is pointless just leaving, at the very same time,
all of these memories.

the attraction between abused animals
as sensed by the strongest.
the swill set before you:
you believe you can feed

my innards exhausted.
the flesh no longer red
the taste having changed. not even
famine will draw you to me

Day 3

he's awake. at each footfall
the asphalt yawns open. he's been bearing for too long
the weight of an oversized body.
his torso sways back and forth,
forcing him into a ridiculous posture.

the tremor of his arms and his head,
the perspiration released,
the trickle of milk oozing up at the joints.

he collects the drops in his cupped hands,
then pours the fluid down his esophagus.
he yanks with his hands at the ends of a wide-opened mouth,
startled as his jaw suddenly locks

Unisex Torso

he was a deformity no more than 13.
with his hands he'd grasp his soft parts.
above
each of them thick lenses were set.
that's how the blind ought to feel: from the umbilicus up –
susurrations of delicate trills;
from the eyelashes down – holy water a-dripping;
from the roots nothing impure ought to spring forth;
13 years
borne on a gigantic torso.

first thing he screamed, then felt around.
behind the vocal chords
something new was afoot.

no further clue.

poplar fluff can ignite. whole piles do catch fire.
over the past few years they've multiplied chaotically.
(not unlike ourselves, there are more females than males in their number.)
he only knew that much:
he was a deformity no more than 13.
with his hands he'd grasp his soft parts.

whenever he'd lose his way he sensed a kind of a darkness
irradiating from his stumps extending with lumps
of plaster carefully rolled out on his chest.
as he moved,
he sensed his fine-grained joints. a puff of white powder afloat in the air,
covering him by degrees.

poplar fluff can ignite. whole piles do catch fire.
over the past few years they've multiplied chaotically.
(not unlike ourselves, there are more females than males in their number.)

he only knew that much:
he was a deformity aged 13 not older.
with his hands he'd grasp his soft parts.

Plaster cast

whenever there is nausea, there is a body, too.
it can no longer be removed from this one.

Interdictions

despite all interdictions, he just wouldn`t stop –
colors his hair white,
wears three quarter pants. never answers, just barks.
he occasionally sits on the lap of a grownup,
studies their moves.
he should burn every note
on the loss of childhood. he mutters:
such blasphemies! while hiding his body.

their hands move in unison, scratch at a blackboard –
the child's body`s at rest, no harder than chalk,
the man's body is tense,
mimics the lines traced by the child.
his eyes are tied, each line
chaotically follows the noise.
it`s neither the right nor the left:
nothing but lost skills

can`t say what is out there.
an instant extension of the body,
a misunderstanding, a primitive writ

his jaw ruminates
calcium and water – components akin to a plaster.
the scratches the man made on the slate extend
into the child's tissues, plunge into the innards.

all around stands a newly-built city

Birds in cages

when the fist movements started
she was barely breathing. she was told
that those were the gestures of a caged bird. two were black,
crawling down. another three were black, holding tight, pushing
each other's bodies.

(breathing hard. rapped something out)

when tissue clung to other tissue flesh began to fall. the smallest
was already naked. agonizing, and her limbs still swayed. pulling
the robust leg of a white bird.

soon above her there was a massive canopy of bodies. rising
instantly as she began waving.

when here there was not anything else,
when here there was not. turning her back
when the bodies rushed in again. covering her,
then besieging her like in a cage. when pushing into one,
the others moved
disjointed.

now she imitates and fists stand. setting down a fake decor of bodies.
their spasms passing in her spasms. their breaths are heard
directly from their lungs. inseminating her lungs, opening

Day 4

the morning ritual, when the knees gathered to the mouth
are fragrant with milk.
at the same time the hair overflows, covers up.
its contact with another's body. the hand drifting
to that place where
a body of a different sort
has been touching the kneecaps.

*

he dissolves 75 mg on the leaf-matted earth
and sniffs.
in the air, the medicine odor.
he brings his head close to the walls of the well,
the tablets descend with a muffled thud,
they're being pulped up along with the compost
he walks by, nods his approval.
he breaks a new blister
and crushes it right upon the rim of the well.
the powder spreads out.
he gathers it back. kneads it all in his hands,
rubs the sides of his head with his forearm. a white stripe
remains on his face, way too little for me, and he sighs.
he presses his palms against each other, he slaps them,
the powder spreads out all around.
he sniffs.
such a waste of time, then he moves in slow motion.
the poison slides down his gullet,
the vocal chords dry up
before he expectorates.

Places

(this place is bad for him.) then
he draws the surroundings like some caved-in roads.
between vital statistics,
between confusions and customs willingly assimilated:
he hasn't seen the light in over a week –
he can easily induce in himself
a state of vertigo.
he goes without food, he talks to no one,
he's careful of manias

he hits every day the same fixed spots,
avoiding lethal areas:
when ebb and tide are controlled from afar,
when inhibitors and stimulants charge.

*

had we but waited together for the change of the signs,
had we but passed as if through a pit covered with dirt
had we but entered halfway.

none of that really happened:
the rocking of wheels at great speed bears
hundreds of thousands like us. a voiceless mob here.

had we but waited together
we might still believe that, us rendered immobile,
this would be the last day.
in the chamber once moist,
two animals might be coming together again.

what is the scream of recognition
what is your voice
today

Day 5

I can see you in a blue light as if you had switched on
a flashlight under the tissues.
switch it off, there is way too much fear.

Diary

he's got the long hair of a woman.

the places he walks through
in between ages, the honey-hued face,
the eyes of a wildcat.

*

whenever he'd turn up he was going the same place –
I'd learned move by move
his back's curvature and his shuffle.
the pale skin as it opens and closes
on members, it lifts up like canvas –
he digs holes for himself in the earth,
palm-sized holes,
stuffs the boulders into his pockets, gathers momentum.

in his wake goes the pounding
of stones rattled up in a jerry can.

he spreads out a jacket onto the earth, he batters it flat. the texture
of rotten leaves. it turns into lignite while he lifts a finger to his mouth, licks
it wet. a new, corpse-like flavor.

(the breath carries away
the unbearable stench)

each morning he wakes up in that state of malaise,
the clang
of a bell striding his trunk. sounds of
a trowel filling up and discharging
a surplus around the head

he pours out in vain, he makes
for the park with the boulders,

lifts up rocks,
he spins on his own in the belfry.

Day 6

he brings his lips to my forehead,
and his lips look as if made from children's skin.
I keep my eyes closed, I open them up
and he comes closer and closer.
he'd like to rummage my temples,
pry them open. to set my eyes to one side,
my hair to the other.

he welcomes me.

streams of water are coming from all sides,
I'm watching those round eyes. wells overflowing
with lime. cold air in my pores, in my eye globes.
I can feel his palm squeezing my neck. next the movement
of his lips on my face. I recognize this closeness.

*

he digs into my gorge. carefully loosens the cuticles;
descends deeper still. the pulsating rhythm of progress,
the unstoppable heat.

in crypts of this kind the asphyxia
possesses the body entirely.

Simulacrum

I need to deduct the sum of our days –
year after year, in a dreary routine – from what has been left.

since the day I met him he's called out in an unvaried pitch,
not exactly coherent at times,
but then ready to trigger
an endless range of female imageries:

I often dream
he's wearing high heels,
ribcage exposed,
all there is to touch
is that bundle of stumps

adorned and summoned
to life by a non-existent body:

a head appended thereon, some sinews
well built, a robust contour.

I want back all that belongs to me

then I let my hands roam all over his stumps,
I encircle his palms (mine),
I encircle his neck (mine),
I watch him from afar.

he continues to wear that odd chunk of body,
that trace of a massacre whose ends he never
finds. he clothes his extremities
in period costume: under their time, in the rancid
odor of those having worn them:
here am I in all
my simulacrum perfection

Day 7

between two bodies gently touching each other,
coarse fur.

Nude

he had fair hair, flaxen hair, jet-black hair,
soft skin he had, scorched skin, heavy skin.

he undid the strands one by one,
took off his skins one by one.
in their absence, the skull.

they were gathered and burnt. carried in garbage sacks.
living creatures sniff the sugary whiff and then urinate.

Day 8

put on your plaster cast once you renounce me. she hesitates,
empties herself of all evil entrails, ready to take him in.

he chooses to do nothing at all. save relieving himself
as he walks. he neither screams, nor does he signal that
something might follow.
he came out of nowhere, no leash and no master.

The Waste Perfect Tense

he'd started talking. fingernails growing out of his gums,
unfurled like ornamental plants
over the cheekbones.
grin, they would say, it's a handicap, they'd protest,
and he'd wait for those late hours of the night:
he'd dress the horn tissues with water, they turned soft, then
they would turn into nooks. it was there he would hide

thoroughly. the best rest's in the places
where no one can find you.

the whole body partook in his rituals: he'd come across something
all his. gaping straight out of the flesh, the caverns.
the tissue would feel, nervures would carve phreatic galleries.
the enamel would fill up the surroundings.
a mountain landscape: the valleys descended
sinuously,
the sky in their wake – then the mouth would snap shut.

horizons turned black,
chasms would gape open.

he made it, I made it, they made it,
he'll make it, I'll make it, they'll make it.

once again he was talking 'bout changes.
'bout the areas meant to stay cut off.
'bout his departure.
he'd invent tales of a realm
he'd have made his way to, rest desired in cages
where no one can find you.

36 days

less than 36 days since we last talked to each other.
by less
than 360 degrees can the body rotate still.
and, there -
when we no longer know.

I had before my eyes the heavy skin.
it had uncovered itself thoroughly,
like some sort of shock-proof wood.
it had developed a sheen and enamel.
it had sunk deep into to the earth

since the earth patch I'm standing on
has the hue of a man's flesh
since my skin's ever whiter

do not wake up. a man's body is attaining perfection.
green wood turns to black wood,
the texture gets rougher.

I'd stir my hands and they'd uncover themselves
I'd press them till neither blood nor the lymph.

then, after a lengthy detour from my own body,
they'd fill up my tissues, they'd lay thick, yet
no induration, nor rubber wood,
but soft wood we can bang on.

you tell me watch out what you dream.
since the earth patch I am standing on
has the hue of a man's flesh
since my skin's ever whiter.

The Return

that's not the way I have imagined the return:

at the end of my foot soles beads of sludge
they're rolling away with each move.

how do all these strangers feel to be dreamt by another,
the straining of arms that hold tight, the new range of whiffs.
last night I perfected the gesture,
I carried it out all the way to the end:

without being given permission I took, I kept hidden away
up into wakefulness.

the roots have stayed on, deeply plunged into the same old turf

no difference between
the breaking of the kneecaps and kneeling.

no difference:
the gestures sought after and the burden of roots

II. Thus Beginneth

Thus Beginneth

they were teeming with water, the mornings he woke up
and rose to his feet; he almost walked over to them,
gave a guttural bark,
birds swept over. they pecked
at the water amassed overnight

he plopped to the ground after turning wild loops in the air,
and knew not whether the start of the day
had to be that way,
all he remembered was that, in place of a mouth,
he carried a huge beak

that such a weight ought to be borne
earthwards,
severely beaten, till it drops off,
till there is a gap left
fit for
an entrance

Cages

he could discern the fluid surfaces
and the aberrant sequence
of flats: they seemed easy to reach:
further life-forms ascend from the very same water
they shoot forth: the landmass surrounded
by fleshy conglomerates; the malodorous scent
of offal stored well past its prime;

he would subdue the body:
the bleedings, the thuds buried deep in the tympani

the very same
shatterproof walls

the rapid motion of fluids upwards, downwards.

salt coagulates tissues
wounds bob with the flotsam;

when they run against dried-up cement
the earth must have dipped below sea level.

Boulders

she was supposed to touch him,
to simulate those steps along with him,
everything she had ever wanted to do.

smile nicely if only she managed to

like a blast from the past:
the shape that his abdomen takes,
that slackness succeeded by tautness.
veins crisscross the legs.
they mime the gigantic anatomy. she detects
her own gestures and handicap.

there's the ghost of a wish:
to be able to sense for a spell the motion in question –
how the tissues come off
to propel him. how she is able to do
all things forbidden to him

The Power

soon as he's got a body
he'd like to be moving, any life form
around yet unformed,
to be breathing along with him.

the power of his stare:
he rotates and retains how he's stared at

soon as he's got a voice
his power:
an unintelligible tremor out of all chests,
the same exhalations, wrung out of the lungs

The Sleep

the things grown at length within nests
where spaces foretell.

the longer they wait with their necks craned,
the expectation of each random noise increases
the intracranial bustle. motions corrode
as they wriggle in soft crania.

thus it happens that they sleep on their feet. liquids
flow in slow motion prompted by heat

*

he only calls him in a cracking voice,
he seems no more than 13,
the warp and weft of organs bears the marks of childhood.
the calves
spread out from underneath furs, uncovering soft kneecaps

when he calls him at all,
his voice becomes the voice of the called one,
the legs kick the nest nervously
they spill way out of it.

Delay

there are no animals here; nor are there any men
with names one can utter just once.
when evil words surface, when words do
get uttered
they are followed by more evil words

winds overflow into the swarms of wasps
scatter them all the way to the mud-squelching ditches;
during their last instants of life
wings sizably thickened with a coating of dirt

prior to any defense.
a body in delay

foretelling a body unformed

*

he casts the blood into the river; bathes
his calves, the skin thereof swells like a sail.
to escape it he dumps earth all over,
he dries it all up.

as he rises, he is wearing the sail round his neck, water
babbling behind:
earth upon earth, life form upon life form,
out of a body lacking symmetry

Figurines

the one wearing a red scarf was him
he walked down the street, from among all the ones walking by I just knew
he had come over to us for the first time.
hands clasped I was standing
behind the rows of long-haired men,
I would squeeze in my fingers a diminutive bell,
I would shake it at each of his steps.

when he would come close enough he would squeezed my palms,
I've recognized you, he'd said.

this odorless city,
with flowers and trees shining bright
with the odorless children and old folks,
with the figurines hid under the Christmas tree.

you are rotating the bell all above us,
walking switches to fast
my eyes follow the flagstones, the inaccurate marks
breeding confusion. I just follow the noise.
I am kneeling before every animal.

the beggars around us,
they wrap us in wool,
the children
scatter all over our heads colored candy,
drape over our shoulders wildcats kept on a leash, we are singing to them,

while the noise, the aseptic-city odor
compel us to panhandle

urge them to come closer
and tell us of the breaths
of far-away cities.

The Mirror

it oughtn't to have started that way.
the space emptied of objects was the first
to bring back to mind. the relaxation of muscles
through their contraction, a spell spent
in front of the mirror
corroding silicon.

*

good milk spills down the arms, at the joints

he wasn't supposed to know he would wind up down there. he would rest
clinging to the thighs of an animal,
he would be touching it at each step.

Crevices

I was in a cage where I practiced new moves:
we watched our organs in mirrors
while unveiling by turns
further pieces of meat.

I said thank you! whenever his members,
whenever the shards whenever my members
displayed muddled pictures

we waited
for nothing but the moments
when
we could look at each other.

thus it was. hours on end when nothing happened: he'd lift up his arms
then wrap them around the trunk,
swaying, touching it.

I kept repeating,

knees knocked against the bars of the cage

The Voice

both of us have our legs way too long:
when you coil them around your body,
I do the same.
(my position is better than yours -
It is all taking place on the left,
I can observe you.)
hands as long as your body, and thin,
trunk swathed in a strip of clean sail

I twiddle my toes without you seeing me.
the screens replay the same endless frame,
the wide-open mouth of a child
twisted by atrocious language.
the gaping jaws and the whites of the eyes.
I've only just felt the devouring is not starting
from there.

today I'll pretend:
every touch is voluntarily guided. we're leaving behind
the abandoned territories

I cannot walk
straight. we are getting into each other's way,
you laugh and your jaws then lock back.
we're seemingly serene, I've got to walk straight:
you can walk.

each of our inclinations,
the most crooked and the purest of them,
a wide-open mouth of a child
twisted by atrocious language.

when you're resting your hand on my shoulder,
when you draw me to you, and my body

is shrinking towards yours.
then the other way round: I can feel the devouring starting
right there.

Delay

day after day some of my limbs desert me.
one hand shrinks and then stretches
it hardly holds me here,
it makes room for me to rush out

III. The Walk

The Walk

here, people walk one behind the other,
their backs supporting the animals' rumps.
knees level with their arms.
a placid procession. the people's backs are
running with white streams.
they're flexing their pecs and the fluid bursts forth.
the prosimians suck at the cascades of milk.
skillful fingers stretch out the white mass
all around nostrils.
it's the milk-fragrant wind trail they follow.

a torso akin to an eye, round and white. moving forth in slow motion,
along the deep trenches. along sharp crunching pebbles.
hard earthen nodules. hard wooden nodules.
all around, expectant torsos.
all ready for advancing, bodies next to the earth.

the torso, white and round.
through it the roads are visible from afar.
hills covered with pebbles come into view.
a discarnate vale and, way down at its end, further vales, neverending.
the torso is writhing in place. the lemurs are the first to slither by.
muzzles awash, they sniff at people's kneecaps.
their mouths close upon them. they bite.
warm milk oozes forth from the kneecaps,
the vales overflow with white curdled waves.
a soothing noise. the lemurs are sleeping,
bodies afloat, halfway into milk.
their fur grows with the abundance of milk.

At night, lemurs and humans glide closer each other.
young bodies steal
past old bodies.
the fragrance of milk changes over to a more pungent fragrance,
the fragrance of wine.
the prosimians sniff. they bite at the wrists.
they bite at the arms that have carried them all that way.

the bodies hang low. giant bellies split open,
on each side of the road.
the carcasses resting.
from afar they appear like heaps of spoiled apples.
on the other side of the road, the fresh corpses.
they look like red apples, fleshy, alive.
a white fluid is seeping through them.
their barely discernible mouths are agape.
their rotund contours.

water bursts out of their nostrils, floods the dry flesh.

on clear days bodies are three-quarter visible.
the shoulders, the thoraxes, the hips, the knees, the soles.
in their wake, bodily chunks hurtle by.
that hair, were it to grow like a weed, would cover them up,
that, consequently,
they'd be three-quarter humans of hair on the move

calls himself lemur mostly on autumn days

I ask him what that means and the answer is easy:
whatever relates to dropping some candy
into some hand. I ask him again and he's like:
today I have run into this powerless beast.
extracted the candy from my mouth
and shoved it under its muzzle, cupped in my hand:
lemur. and then? what did it do? its hair was not yet grown.
it had wooden knots at the joints of its feet.
what next? it breathed into my face.
it smoothed the piece of candy with its muzzle – it didn't care for it.
after retrieving it,
I felt it all different on my palate.
its taste was akin to its smell. it went on breathing,wraiths of white steam
spreading round its muzzle.

he recognizes me by my white torso.
he lies down in the new grass I'm leading him to.
he's got big blue eyes. he is not yet a lemur.
he goes wherever. we could have walked to the forest
that ends in a chasm.
he said: it's your choice. I chose at random,
unaware he was going to change into a lemur.
we're walking downhill. he follows me smiling,
in a black fur almost making a cover.
we run, I whistle. we can't see a thing. we call out.
the sound fades away in the apple-tree orchard.
in the chestnut-tree orchard.
in the orchard with houses on the point of collapsing.
crouching down feels so good at diminutive height.
we breathe the warm air now leaving our nostrils.
the lemur leans down on his front paws increasingly harder,
leaning towards me as he mirrors my gesture.

that white torso between us.
that's the torso he's anxious to feel.

on the right, a small heap of rotten apples,
on the left, a small heap of ripe apples

at night he's afraid of the body. in the dark, he tells me,
he can see just whatever is white.
he tells me my eyes would do him good. as he departs,
he rubs his hands in the black dust.
raises them to his eyelids.
the blue eyes rush to my blue eyes:
we won't see each other ever again.

the winding up

the twine grows all around the woods.
sharp nails grow all around the table.
I am stretching myself and, from the opposite end, you wind up the slack.
you touch, wind me up.
the scrapings yield nothing but rust.

Malaise

I turn the lemur's head, so as to be facing the grassland.
his eyes will thus rest.
I will then allow them to shake the grass off
and dry up as if in the plain.

Poison

he picks me up in his arms
and carries me next to the windows.
we're high up in the air. here, next to the windows,
there is nothing at all. everything's been abandoned.

when he says poison, my arms are trickling with
a glutinous liquid.
nerves, muscles, contractions, he says.
he's feeling my joints with his tongue, then he spins
with me through the white light of the hall.

we are feeling the skin of each other's warm palms.
whenever I want anything, he wants it himself,
whenever I say anything, he has already said it,
whenever I'm sick, he has already seen a concrete wall
allowing no passage.

*

he comes loose off my body, does the rounds of the others.
from the edge of my bed, I kick off the sheets and cry out.

New

you're unripe,
in a beautiful house, after a long, long time. it has barely come to an end –
the filling up of empty objects with full ones, they've been barely removed –
the old edges. in perfect cleanliness, their subdued laughter,
their walking on tiptoes. at each of my footfalls they rear
their heads. they stretch themselves on my chest as the heart straightens itself
like an old man in a desert. that's where I stay with them when
the midday sun shines its brightest.
their muzzles warm, ask to change my unbreathable air.

I breathe into their nostrils, they carry on the breeze.
here's where the arid lands come to an end.

in a lovely house I have no time
to roam. nor time to wait, to lay my hand
upon your heads, to feel the tender texture of your fur.
I only have the time to move along, to close the brand-new doors,
to scatter the ancient dry edges
with fruit pulped in my fist, as if
the craving flaring up for tender bodies
has come to an end

The Basement

upon his legs. then underneath them.
the vertebrae slid
upon the skin surface. they spread something already empty,
a carcass that, had you but turned it around,
you could have seen it:
a nude felid; an enormous disemboweled animal;
a man with the organs exposed,
then sounds issuing from the bowels of a porcelain
machine. its skin white and soft,
the veins discernible all over the surface of the body.
a motion or two
and I would have continued. (I furtively glanced – as I entered
there were plaster-of-paris prints on the floor – the footprints did not
continue)

sex&crime&punishment. carves in an abandoned basement,
like into prison walls.
props of a children's ball,
the play with oversized objects. the tunnel of fear
all along the banisters leading in any given direction.

legs in circular motion, never stopping,
visible from afar. he'd like to get hold of a brick with them,
now they coil round the neck. for a few
moments he wavers, doesn't lob it towards the windows,
rests it behind them.

Copper

from one side

it appeared that all his motions turned right
then sank into a rhythm anything but intense.

a scaly chunk of wood
that one's come from the south
therefore I must follow
the way of the north,
he came off root an' all, knots
and threads smeared all over. as he moves he scrapes against gentle planes.
he comes to a halt.
next, from the left, a warm gust is coming, getting close,
the tremor is lascivious, naughty they call him
and joints stop allowing themselves to be engulfed
by the soothing air.

once again he crosses the tracks
and the numbering becomes reversed. the only point of balance
between intersections could be there.
between his white palms and her white palms.

then the highest building. the body
and her, taking turns.
then the vague wrought-iron shapes.

as if he had been called, he unwinds,
he can go anywhere, this precious
dizziness, almost resembles the last
cardiac spasms, and once again the crisscrossing of
ligaments akin to the intersection
of copper tracks.

XXX

he stands up and looks left, hearing nothing,
then looks right without seeing:
in order not to grasp him with both hands,
I will not find him. all he does is make a move
like any other.

*

astroporexmirjelumicarx. that's about all I have to say.

*

she stretches her body, pulls up her dress and comes in.
she's removed all the bars.
such a beautiful being;
he's watching her for a second or two. does nothing,
listens to the rhythm of her breath. ever so light yet steady.
he can't see her face, though he could tell she has fallen asleep.
she's at peace, it's in her that he startles.

*

I'm telling you, just like a frenzied flower.
stop getting any closer, it withers.
that's getting you nowhere.

*

she's closed her eyes. opens them up.
she's closed her eyes. opens them up.
a giant lantern's blue light
hanging above them. she closes her eyes. stops.
a break.
there, keep it up, it's alright, that's where fear disappears.

The Place

you asked what it was like out there. no idea.
I was outside some courtyard,
then at the end of some road.
the street names and metal signs left in place.

you asked what it was like out there. no idea.
a place we could have made our way to,
with people
descended half way

*

in order to move wherever he pleased
he'd prop up his shoulders with sticks and shuffle away
with minced steps.

– his gait took the shape
of his body, a crippled progress
made harder by the dust gathered under his soles

he sniffs at the air, as he decides on the right course,
the trails left by animals
ahead of him –

*

the skin of your face is rough as soon as it's morning.
hammers strike steadily,
they uncover the bones, the lacrimal grottos, they wreck.
then the cranium
surfaces.

I recognize you fully:
gentle features, allowing nothing to be kept,
the promise of this (sur)facing

The Torso

the rounded white torso constantly shows me the way.
today we are not going back to our house. after a two days' walk,
the house seems to be too far behind. the house is all taken apart.
the roof has spilled over under the weight of the leaves
covering it. it has stretched out its timber,
all over the valley. it's resting them as if they were arms.

when feeding the torso I'm feeding wet mouths.
the peering muzzles harbor misshapen teeth.
they have been crushing bony carcasses.
in the hairs of their fur
milk laces abide. evening after evening,
in the wide-open bellies of prosimians
the shivering bodies of humans took shelter.
night after night, in the wide-open bellies of houses,
other shivering bodies took shelter.

in the afternoon it's corpse-gathering time. the dried stalks
of wild roses. rotten parasite plants.
brown mushrooms and poisonous ones.
deep ditches are being dug. shovels crush the earth,
grinding it.
young bodies bounce all around the ditches.
walls bounce all around the ditches.
they all take shelter, they pour the earth back in place.
here and there, barely visible muzzles breathe the air that comes from all
over.

Infant Walkers

I took my first steps with infant walkers,
with catgut
was I lifted from the ground

the good milk, the lace
of animals with shot-ridden chests,
with carcass fur, for the briefest of spells
they kept my eyes open
to watch straight ahead.

I suckled on, trusting
that would be all,
after bipedal walking replaced
hands-forward progress.

out of animal membranes I perfected
human membranes.

sparkling scales grow along with the body.
with eyelids squeezed tight,
with nostrils filled up
the good milk turns to bad milk,
liquid earth turns to hard earth.

I was borne on a vast fur
upon the shoulders of beings with
faces covered in plaster.

the absence of vision replaced
the absence of hands replaced
the absence of legs.

*

we want to recover and then say that eyes
tumefied prevent us from looking around.

they open for a few seconds a day, the sight
of such a distorted face
brings along:
the carcass stench, the contracted abdominal muscles

reflex and excitation hurt alike

The Departure

I could not talk.
then I kept my mouth wide open.
its elongated forms pulled both sides of the face.
the animal thumps me furiously, it pants.
it snaps its own vertebrae against my hard bones

out of the head tissue hair is beginning to crackle.
waves white with milk are flooding the forehead. fever. poison.
the noise of bodies getting stiff.
first the back. the vertebrae bend.
the legs crawl sideways.
fever in the eyes, under the skin.
lemur, I scream while milk softens the vocal cords.

unfed, the mouths continue to scream.

*

we cover ourselves, frenzy is gone.

they battered with their fists, they gathered us all at once,
they picked up the stumps.

we persistently quiver
in familiar flesh.

and lo, for the very first time,
the milk is ebbing from us,
an evil blood
in long-time familiar bodies.

I woke up surrounded by them, they were pulling my hair,
as if each of my hairs had to be twisted. then the commotion
all over my forehead, they were struggling to reach my eyelashes.
I did not open my eyes, stayed like that for a second or two.
the same warm familiar breath all around me.
they were whispering lemur. I whispered along, felt
the name tickling my vocal cords,
felt the bed sheet. it was warm, it was soft,
all around my ankles. I could not move.
the wet muzzles stuck to my nostrils were breathing my
air. today my voice is so soft,
it almost slides from my throat to my chest,
it is beautiful.

A new body

night after night I mistreat my voice.
I press my hands to my throat, stretching my skin,
pulling at it.

the guttural sound of barking.

*

his body as good as new. he appears to have crossed a river.
the wet fur, almost frozen.
I thought he had vanished.

I show him the marks round my neck,
so that he sees how frightened I have been.

he's got glassy eyes.
he's reaching with his muzzle for my arms.
tells me to take his head into my hands.
lay his neck upon mine. lemur, I whisper.
his fur is covered in blood.
he went with some beast not so long ago, dragged it over the fields.

I touch my fingers, my skin tastes of him.
for hours on end the blood has taken shelter under nails.
the unchanged tang the two of us have tasted at the same time
and the beast that he killed.

I'm striking my fingers against the walls, the stairs, the table.
there's not one drop of harmony.
minute white beads converge around the mouth.

at night I leave my house. I walk closer to them,
the bodies move aside. I have reduced their rations,
I have kept their hunger keen
.so they recognize each other from afar, like living prey.

through opaque air I cannot make my way.
not even milk shines here in the night time.
the congealed tracks look like the trails of animals
that crept underground.

small bodies I lay on the colored side.
big ones, on the colorless side.

haven't seen him for days.
I leave food for him on the porch,
I'm enticing him. never ask whether anyone's seen him.
since he's left, the voice is once again soft,
I feel as if dozens of eggs have broken
over the vocal cords. they've become viscid.

Stops

whenever he moves away, I wrap my neck
in a scarf,
I stop the sounds from emerging.

the calls of other animals are heard from outside.
I don't open the shutters, roars keep their own vigil.

Silence

he broke free from the worst of all places and moved on.
towards noon the distance from members to the sky
is so narrow
that eyes are filling with the crumb of fresh loaves.

that isn't sleep,
a beast bleats in the distance; reaching for it, light pierces the thicket mile
after mile.

*

he'd wrapped a length of cloth around his neck to hear himself no more
while watching the gestures of females
and the pups they were cradling.

whenever the wind blew, the membrane would come loose from his neck
– they'd be ten times louder within their tanned hides –

he would just squat and wait,
while rolling in his palms the soft alveoli
until they gave way.
the welding between them appeared to be eroded in those moments

when
he was driving
the first beings
silencewards

APPENDIX

THERE WAS AS YET NO INDICATION that a body would come into being, that it would move. No gestures existed for the entity I was creating. But at a residency in the part of the world were *The Shining* was shot—in one of the most artistic regions of the US, Portland, Oregon— I by chance met a choreographer whose language seemed to draw from the same movie as my Lemur character. We conjured the entity using my voice and Romanian language without translation. We seemed to create and complete a Lemur from ground zero, a Frankenstein's creature who exceeded our expectations. Out of nothing, a ghostly voice arose and became Poetry and Choreography.

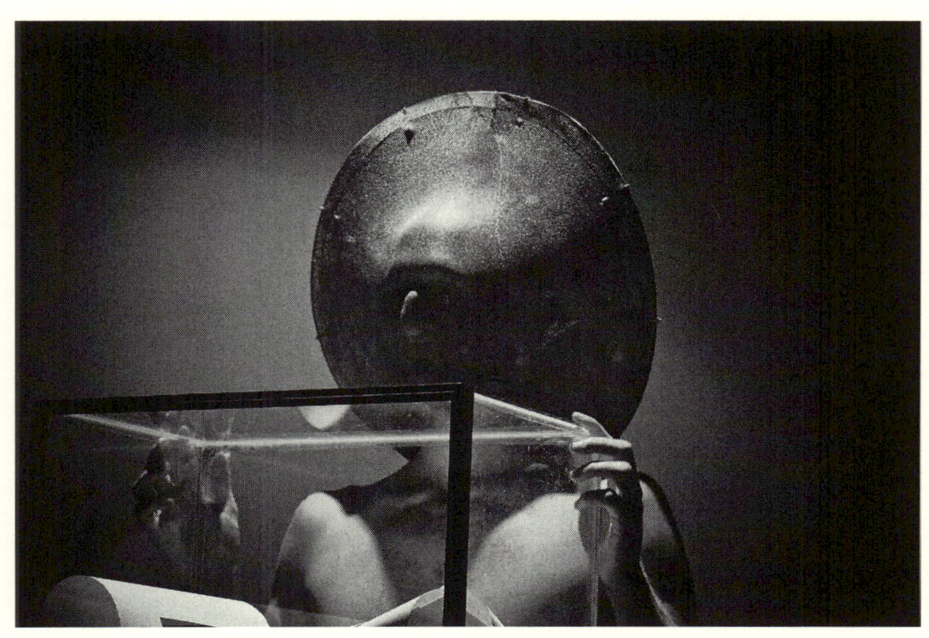

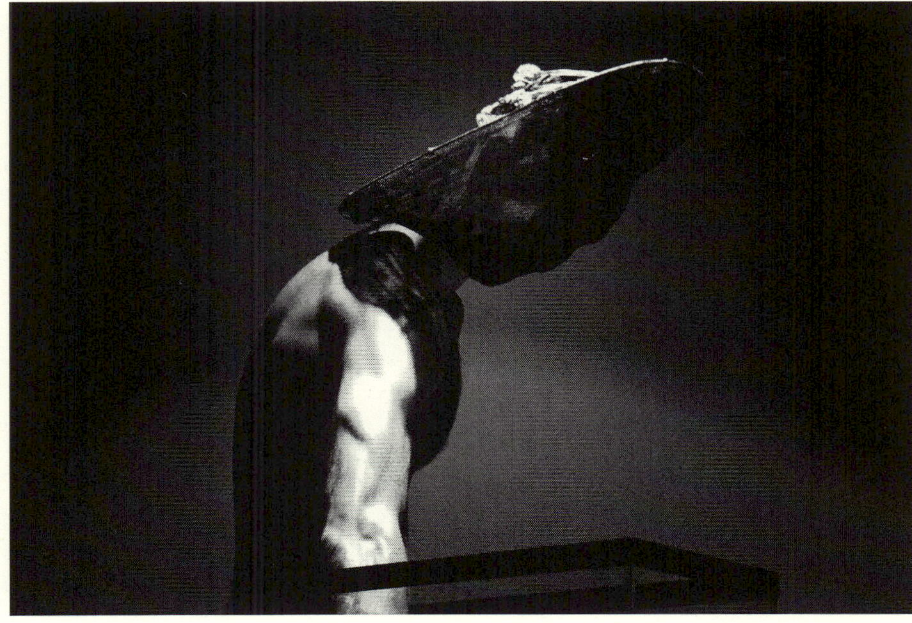

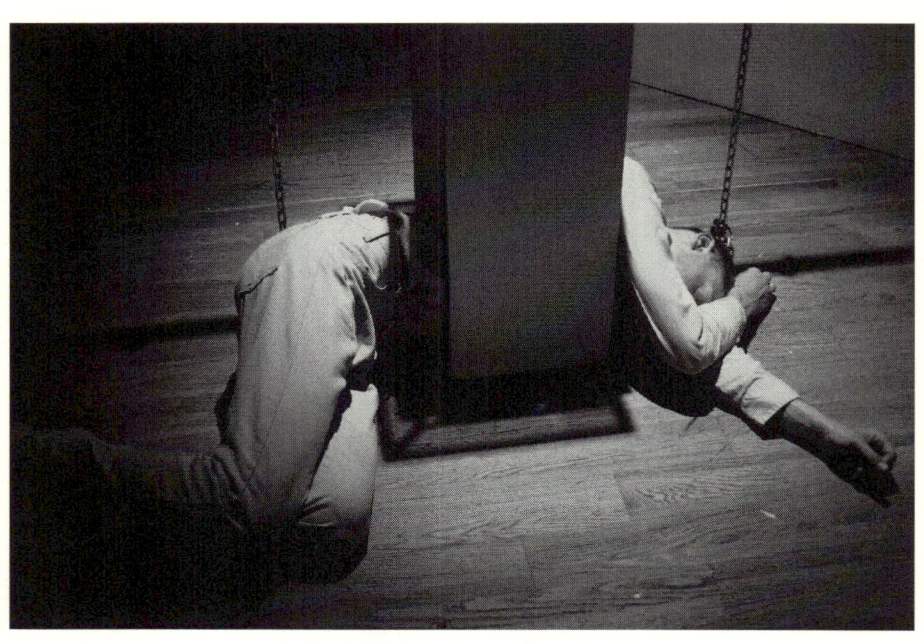

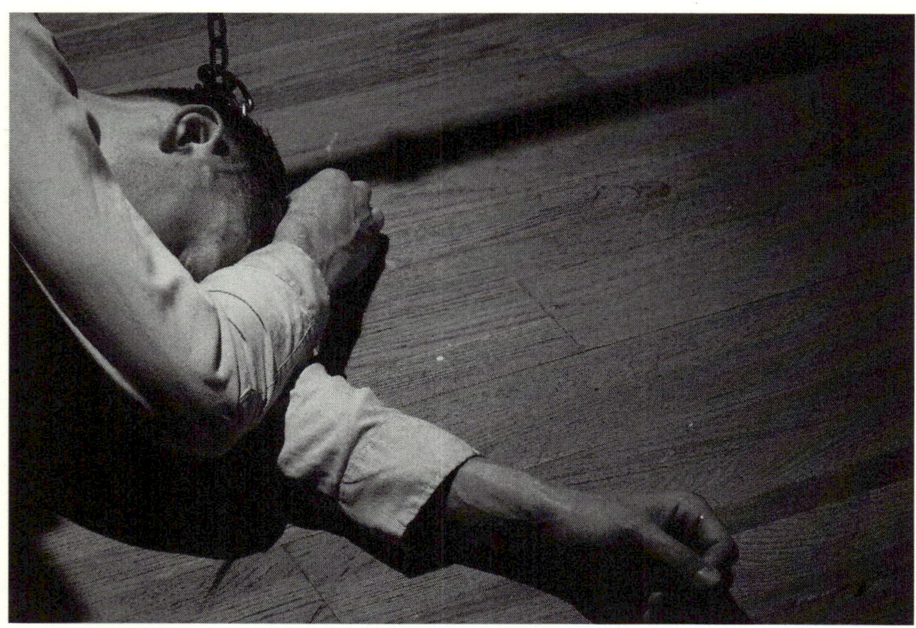

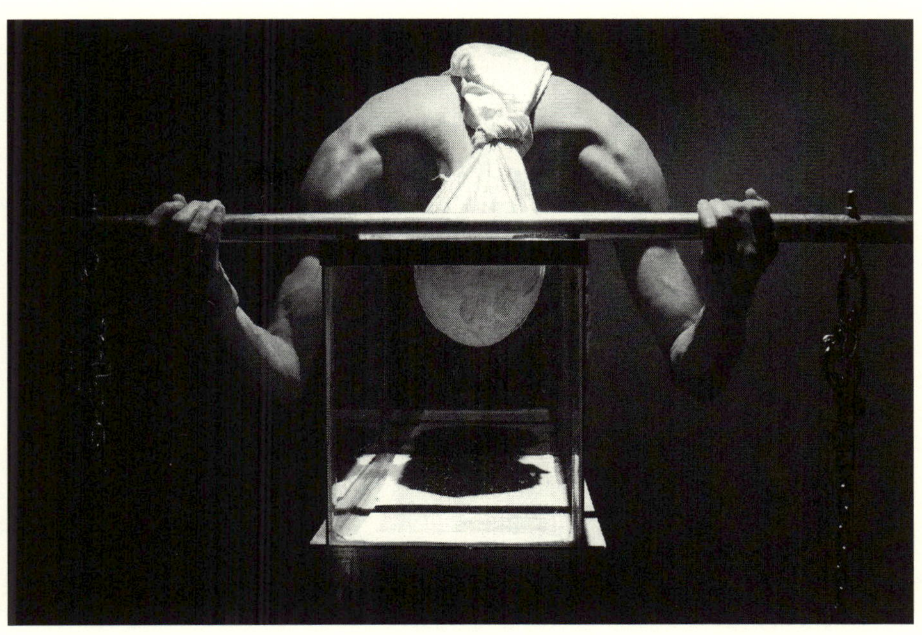

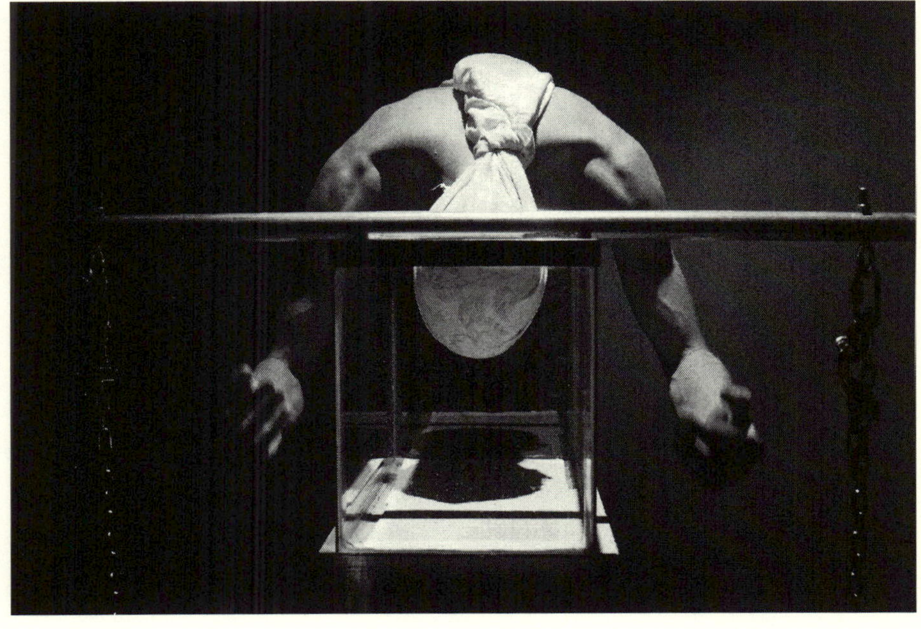

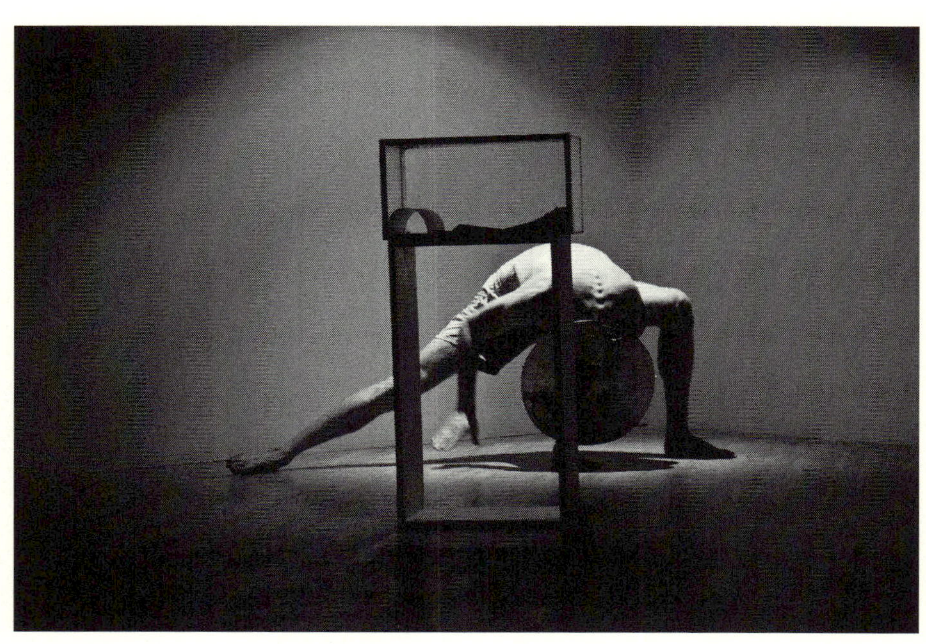

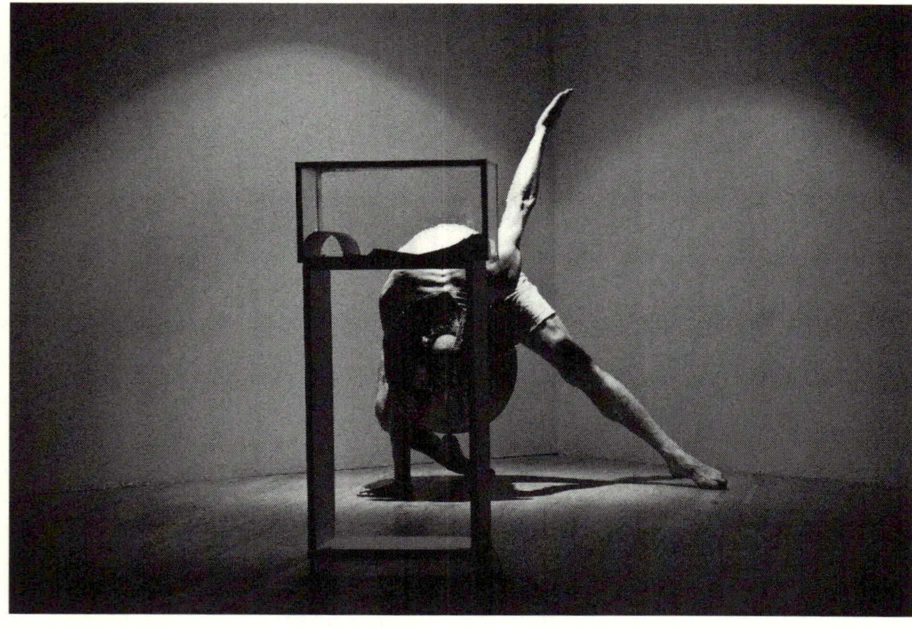

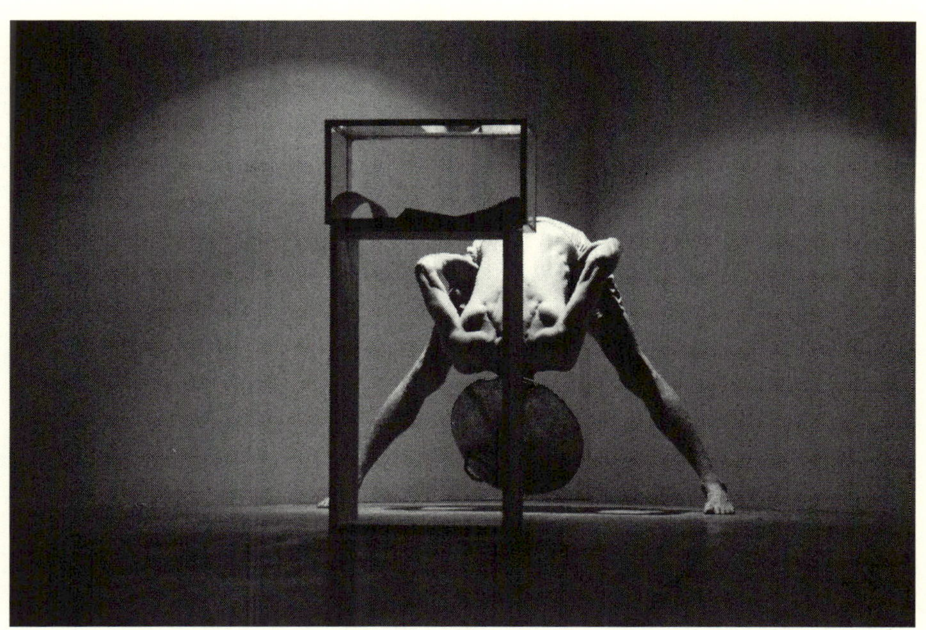

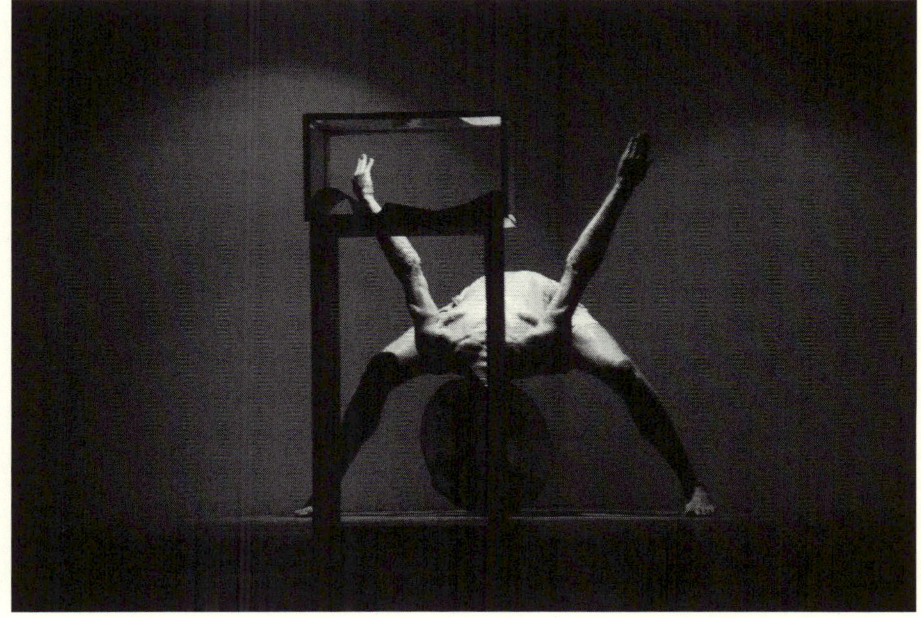

Andra Rotaru is a poet and the founder of the multimedial and multilingual journal Crevice. Her dance performance Lemur has been performed in the US and across Europe together with the choreographer Robert Tyree. She has worked extensively at the intersection of poetry, fiction, photography, video and performance. She is the author of *Într-un pat sub cearșaful alb* (*In a Bed Under the White Sheet*, 2005); *En una cama bajo la sábana blanca* (the Spanish translation of her debut volume, 2008); *Ținuturile sudului* (*Southern Lands*, 2010); and *Lemur* (2012). Rotaru was awarded The Best Young Poet of Year Award at The Writers' Gala in Bucharest (2013) for *Lemur*. A selection of her poems in Anca Roncea`s translation won Asymptote`s Close Approximations Prize in 2017 (judged by Sawako Nakayasu).

Florin Bican studied English at the University of Bucharest, Romania, where he became a compulsive translator of Romanian literature. His translations have been published in Britain, Ireland, the United States, Singapore and Romania. His translations from English into Romanian include Lewis Carroll's *The Hunting of the Snark* and T.S. Eliot's *Old Possum's Book of Practical Cats*. When not translating, Bican writes articles for British and American magazines and works on subversive children's literature. His first volume of poetry, *A Slob's Treasury of Verse* (Bucharest, 2007), is a collection of politically incorrect cautionary rhymes. His work-in-progress, *Torpid Tropics*, is an attempt at cautionary prose, and just as politically incorrect. In 2009 he edited and contributed to *The Cook-a-Book Pancyclopedia of Texts and Images*, an anthology of Romanian children's literature. From 2006 onwards, Bican was in charge of the Romanian Cultural Institute program *Translators in the Making*, training foreign students to translate Romanian literature into their respective languages, until the program collapsed under government pressure. In May 2013, he published his second volume of unorthodox children's poetry *The Recyclopedia of Rhyming Nonsense*.

ROBERT TYREE is a choreographer, educator and web developer based London, England with roots in Portland, Oregon.

Robert has trained at the University of Washington, Montréal's after-hours clubs, Oregon Ballet Theatre and Vienna's danceWEB program at ImPulzTanz.

His earliest work pursued a concept of intensive dance through performance and publication. Discos with Deleuze, lofting with Lacan—basically club dancing meets critical theory. This culminated in the all-ages All-Night Dance as well as the design + discourse chapbook Intensive Dance. Another series of work paired blogging and dance for video with an enigmatic, improvised solo. This two-year collaboration with Romanian poet Andra Rotaru shared a mutually imagined character, Lemur.

Tyree has worked with several choreographers in Portland including Tahni Holt, Linda Austin, Lucy Lee Yim, Pepper Pepper, and Meshi Chavez.

Tyree is co-instigator of FRONT, a Portland-based newspaper devoted to fostering dialogs and literacy around contemporary dance. Additionally, his performance writings have been published online through outlets including Claudia La Rocco's Performance Club and the Portland Institute for Contemporary Art.